IN THEIR OWN VOICES

Young People's Letters
to the
President

by Judith E. Greenberg

Franklin Watts
A Division of Grolier Publishing
New York   London   Hong Kong   Sydney
Danbury, Connecticut

Photographs ©: AP/Wide World Photos: 87 (Mark Wilson), 12, 30, 39, 55; Archive Photos: 68; Chamber of Commerce, Austin, Texas: 53; Corbis-Bettmann: 3, 19, 28 bottom; Dwight D. Eisenhower Library: 38; Folio, Inc.: 15 (W. Mcnamee), 17 (Pete Souza), 57; Franklin Watts File: cover bottom center, 21, 44, 61; Harry S. Truman Library: 34, 35; John F. Kennedy Library: 45; Library of Congress: cover top left, 8 left (Alex Gardner) 10, 52; National Archives and Records Administration: 28 top; National Park Service, Washington, D.C.: 36; Presidential Center: 13; Reuters/Archive Photos: cover bottom right, 80 (Luc Novovitch); The Lincoln Museum, Fort Wayne, IN.: 8 right (Burton Historical Collection); UPI/Corbis-Bettmann: cover bottom left, 22, 41, 64, 74; Washington Convention and Visitors Bureau: 14.

Visit Franklin Watts on the Internet at:
http://publishing.grolier.com

Library of Congress Cataloging-in-Publication Data

    Greenberg, Judith E.
    Young people's letters to the president / by Judith E. Greenberg.
      p. cm. — (In their own voices)
    Includes bibliographical references and index.
    Summary: A selection of letters written to United States presidents by children and youths; includes historical background material to provide a context for the writers' concerns and ideas.
     ISBN 0-531-11435-X
    1. Presidents — United States — Correspondence — Juvenile literature.
    2. Children — United States — Correspondence — Juvenile literature.
    3. United States — Politics and government — 20th century — Juvenile literature. 4. Children's writings, American — Juvenile literature.
    [1. Presidents — Correspondence. 2. United States — Politics and government — 20th century. 3. Children's writings. 4. Youth's writings.]   I. Title. II. Series.
    E176.1.G825 1998
    973'.083 — dc21   97-51202
                                                      CIP
                                                          AC

GROLIER
PUBLISHING

To Julian Bond: Ideas are wonderful, especially when they are generously shared. Thank you for the inspiration.   *J.E.G.*

A special thank-you to Beth Haverkamp, currently at the U.S. Holocaust Museum, Washington, D.C., and previously an educational consultant at the National Archives. Her research work was invaluable, as was her dedication to seeing that this book was written and published.

The president's mailing address is:
The President
The White House
Washington, D.C. 20500

Contents

chapter 1
Save that Letter!

Each week, President Bill Clinton receives eight to nine thousand letters from young people, and that doesn't include a large number of E-mail letters! Students often write to the president as part of a social studies homework assignment. Young people write to say "congratulations" on being elected or "I hope you are feeling better." Many of the writers wish to discuss serious political issues—campaign financing, affirmative action, or censorship. Some write about current events, or ideals, such as patriotism. Others just want to know if the White House pet has Secret Service agents.

Whatever the content, every letter is read, saved, and cataloged. Each letter is a piece of history, which will tell future readers something about Clinton, his family, his politics, his country, and about the times in which he lived and served the country as president.

A sampling of the letters are sent to the president weekly, for him to read and choose some to answer. Eventually these letters will be housed in Clinton's presidential library, and scholars will be able to study them.

Writing to the president of the United States is part of our democratic heritage. In our country, we can write to the president and speak freely, saying things that other countries might not allow. In America, we are free to voice our opinions and even offer advice to the president!

For example, in a famous letter written by an eleven-year-old girl, Grace Bedell, to President Lincoln, she suggested that perhaps he wouldn't look so thin and tired if he grew a beard to cover his face and make it look fuller. He liked the idea and did grow the beard. In fact he wore a beard from that time on!

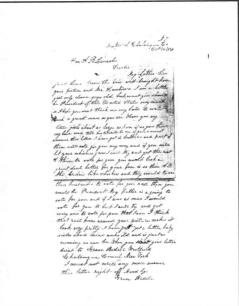

President Abraham Lincoln's gaunt face prompted a suggestion from a letter writer.

NY
Westfield Chatauque Co
Oct 15. 1860

Hon A B Lincoln
Dear Sir
    My father has just [come] home from the fair and brought home your picture and Mr. [Hannibal] Hamlin's [Lincoln's running mate]. I am a little girl only eleven years old, but want you should be President of the United States very much so I hope you won't think me very bold to write to such a great man as you are. Have you any little girls about as large as I am if so give them my love and tell her to write to me if you cannot answer this letter. I have got 4 brother's and part of them will vote for you any way and if you will let your whiskers grow I will try and get the rest of them to vote for you you would look a great deal better for your face is so thin. All the ladies like whiskers and they would tease their husband's to vote for you and if I was a man I would vote for you to but I will try and get every one to vote for you that I can   I think that rail fence around your picture makes it look very pretty. I have got a little baby sister she is nine weeks old and is just as cunning as can be. When you direct your letter dir[e]ct to Grace Bedell Westfield Chatauque County New York
    I must not write any more answer this letter right off Good bye
Grace Bedell

Three months later, Lincoln was on a train traveling to Washington, D.C., for his inauguration. When he reached the stop at Westfield, New York, Grace's hometown, crowds came out to greet him. Lincoln asked to see the little girl who had helped his appearance. When he spotted her, Lincoln walked over and kissed her on the cheek, thus making Grace and her letter forever famous.

The tradition of writing letters to the president as a class assignment began as early as 1877, as seen in the letter on the next page to President Rutherford B. Hayes. Hayes received many congratulatory letters, perhaps because his election was not certain until the last minute. The election was disputed, and a special commission had to decide the winner, and thus new president. His wife, Lucy Hayes, left their home in Ohio to come to the inauguration before anyone was sure who would be the new president. Hayes was declared the winner, but another problem arose. President Ulysses S. Grant was to leave office on the evening of Saturday, March 3, 1877. Hayes was due to be sworn in on Mon-

President Rutherford B. Hayes

day, March 5. This would leave the country without a leader for more than a day. Grant solved the problem by arranging a private swearing-in ceremony for the new president at 12:01 A.M. on Sunday, March 4. One minute after Grant left office,

Mt. Carroll Illinois
Feb 7 1877

Hon. R. B. Hayes
Columbus Ohio

Sir
    It affords me great pleasure to have the honor to congratulate you upon the splendid run you have made for the Presidency of the United States. As I know, will you succeed in getting the office you will ably perform its duties. Again congratulations you I remain

Very Respectfully

Nettie B. Moore

P.S.   I am a little girl 13 years old. I am attending school and I am a Republican.

The inauguration of Rutherford B. Hayes

the ceremony took place in the Red Room of the White House with only a few people attending. The public ceremony was on Monday, followed by a torchlight parade to celebrate the new president.

Hayes received many letters of congratulation, but also many asking for money or jobs, or just old clothes. The Civil War had ended only twelve years earlier, and the economy was not yet very strong. Many people, especially in the South, were still finding it difficult to get work. Lucy Hayes, too, received so many letters that she was the first president's wife to have a secretary to help her read and answer them.

Letters to President Hayes and his papers are preserved in this library at his home, Spiegel Grove, in Fremont, Ohio.

Hayes was president before the system of presidential libraries was created by the United States government. His letters, Civil War memorabilia, and presidential papers are housed in the excellent Rutherford B. Hayes Presidential Center in Fremont, Ohio, his home of many years.

President Herbert C. Hoover was the first president to have a library built to house his presidential papers. Every succeeding president has had a library built for his papers, but the Richard Nixon library is privately run. The George Bush library was recently opened on the campus of Texas A & M University, which also houses the Bush School of Government and Public Service.

The vast collections of the Library of Congress include presidential papers and historical documents and are open to all citizens of the United States.

The letters in this book were written by young people to presidents. The writers express their feelings about their times and the issues that are important to them. The letters cover the time from President Hoover to President Clinton, as they are all part of the Presidential Library Act.

These letters to the president are primary source material. They offer eyewitness accounts of life. As in a diary or a journal, the young writers often speak directly, telling the president just what they are thinking. Some beg for help with an issue that is national, but still very personal to that letter writer. The letters tell the story of the American presidency

An interior view of the Library of Congress

through the eyes of the young writers. Many of the writers express themselves well, and their letters show their courage, fears, and sincere feelings about issues such as desegregation. Others that are lighter, or even funny, were still saved and answered. They too are pieces of history and contain someone's honest feelings. These young people's letters also help us learn about the public's understanding of the people who were president.

The language and subject matter of these letters reflect the period in which they were written. Some were written by young children, as can be seen in their words, expressions, and handwriting. We have not altered any of the letters and remind readers that they present the feelings, beliefs, and prejudices of the writer's own times.

Many of the letters we have selected were read by the president and were answered either personally by him or by an aide. Some answers are included in the book and demonstrate that young writers are not ignored but are taken seriously by the president and the president's staff. Each letter is a small piece of history sitting on a page for you to examine and use, to better understand an event, a person, or a time in America's history. The letters are presented in chronological order to better help you understand the historical period of each letter.

A list of presidential centers and sites is included in an appendix. A list of presidental libraries with addresses and phone numbers is also included, and you can contact any of these libraries for more information. The letters and papers of the presidents prior to Hoover can also be found in the National Archives or the Library of Congress in Washington, D.C. Microfilm copies are available to the public for reading and study. Some of the early presidential centers lack the funds for full staffs; some do not even have historians or curators to take care of the letters. It is thus even more important and fortunate that these particular presidential papers can be found in the Library of Congress.

Your own letters to the president, like the ones you are about to read, can also become a part of history. They might possibly be read and studied by students and historians years from now.

An interior view of the National Archives, where many of the letters and papers of past presidents are stored

17

chapter 2
Hoovervilles and a Case of Polio

The world of President Herbert Hoover fell apart just seven months after he took office in 1929. During his presidency, the Great Depression began, a time when many American businesses failed and millions of workers lost their jobs. Wealthy businesspeople lost their fortunes and average citizens lost their life savings and then their jobs after the stock market crashed on October 29, 1929. The people looked to Hoover and the government to help them save their businesses, find work, or provide money for food and housing. Hoover, a Republican, didn't want to interfere with the economy. Like most people at that time, he believed the economy would recover on its own. He felt labor and industry should solve their own problems.

At this time there were 48 states in the Union and the country's population was 121,767,000. At the start of Hoover's presidency, many Americans had been enjoying prosperity and living well. Others, however, were not as fortunate. Farmers, coal miners, and textile workers were earning very low wages and working in terrible conditions. The economy was also weaker than it seemed. Businesses were producing more products than consumers could buy. Many people were buying on credit and didn't have the cash to pay their debts. The economy was practically doomed to fail, but Hoover did not want to take action. As the depression deepened, some people became so desperate and poor that they lived in cardboard shacks. "Hoovervilles"—communities of penniless, unemployed people—appeared in many urban areas. Unemployed American workers staged hunger marches and demonstrations in cities throughout the nation during the

"Hoovervilles" sprang up in many locations during the Great Depression. Here the scene is Central Park in New York City.

early 1930s. The most famous was the Bonus Army, which was made up of World War I veterans who wanted the government to pay them money they had been promised for military service.

The letter to Hoover from Barbara Jane McIntyre shows that young people were worried about the conditions in the nation and tried to help as best they could. Hoover's reply was kind, but if we read it carefully, we may see the shortsightedness of his efforts to end the depression. Perhaps the job of

Nov. 10, 1931.

Dear President Hoover:
I, Barbara McIntyre 10. years old, my girl friends and I have made a good plan for the poor people this winter. Here it is, see how you like it. Well we are going to get old blankets and cloths, shoes and food and we are going to send it to you and for you to send it to poor. We are taking up a collection and every week we get a penny to a dime, every time and we are having a lot of fun this year. This is the first year we have ever done this and we expect to do it every year.

Yours Sincerly,
Barbara Jane McIntyre
516 Piedmont Road,
Columbus Ohio

November 19, 1931.

Miss Barbara Jane McIntyre,
516 Piedmont Road,
Columbus, Ohio.

My dear Barbara:
    I have your very sweet letter of November 10th. It is a very beautiful undertaking. I would suggest, however, that instead of sending the contributions which you collect to me that you should yourself distribute them to those who are in need in your own locality.

Yours faithfully,

(Herbert Hoover)

President Herbert Hoover

turning the economy around was too great for a president who seemed shy and quiet and thought people should not need government help.

By 1932, the Republicans had little hope that Hoover and his vice president, Charles Curtis, would be reelected. In fact, they were soundly defeated by Democrats Franklin D. Roosevelt and John N. Garner, who won 42 of the 48 states. The whole nation hoped and prayed that the new president would be able to end the depression.

Roosevelt took office on March 4, 1933, when he was fifty-one years old, determined to solve the country's economic

President Franklin Roosevelt often spoke directly to the public by radio.

problems. By this time, people were drawing their last savings out of banks to pay their bills. The banks ran out of money and shut their doors. Roosevelt closed all the banks and declared a "bank holiday." This gave the Treasury time to examine the banks' records and determine which were in good shape and which should be closed permanently. This action helped restore faith in the American banking system, and people started to put any money they could save back into the reopened banks.

Roosevelt also sent Congress proposals for new bills to strengthen the economy and help needy Americans. Most were passed, including the Agricultural Adjustment Act, the Tennessee Valley Authority Act, the Social Security Act, and the National Industrial Recovery Act. These bills created new organizations that put people to work, gave help to troubled industries, constructed public buildings, and offered aid to elderly, retired, and disabled people. Roosevelt called these programs the "New Deal." He also spoke to the nation by radio in "fireside chats." During these informal talks he explained the actions he and the government were taking and what he planned for the future. The chats helped Americans regain their faith in the country and the government.

Roosevelt was elected president a total of four times. By his third election, most of Europe and Asia was at war. The United States slowly became involved in World War II, supplying food and arms to the Allied nations fighting against Germany, Italy, and Japan—the Axis powers. The Japanese attacked the U.S. naval base at Pearl Harbor on Sunday, December 7, 1941, and the U.S. Congress declared war the next day. The United States became one of the "Big Three," joining England and Russia in fighting against the Axis powers.

Throughout Franklin D. Roosevelt's years as president, he was often photographed for newspapers and filmed for movie newsreels, but the photographs did not reveal that the nation's leader could not walk without assistance. He was rarely shown with his leg braces or sitting in a wheelchair. In 1921, Roosevelt had suffered an accident while sailing. He fell into the icy water and became very chilled. Although help reached him quickly, Roosevelt was in severe pain and soon his entire body was paralyzed. He developed polio, a disease caused by a tiny virus that attacks the brain and spinal cord. The virus multiplies quickly and paralysis can occur if many

May the 6th.
2135 No. 67th St.
St. Louis. Mo.

Mr. President:
Wash, D.C.
    I am a little boy eleven years old. I, like you have infantile payelisis since I was 14 months old. Just in my right limb and right side. I have to go to the hospital in about 6 weeks for 2 operations, and the Dr. says stay 3 months. that will be my whole vacatoin when school is over. But maybe it will be best for me. I will close I listen to the radio.

from Harold Hancock

cells are destroyed. It wasn't until 1955 that the first polio vaccine was created by Jonas E. Salk and given to children by injection. By 1961 Albert B. Sabin had developed a vaccine that could be swallowed, but these were too late for Franklin Roosevelt.

Although paralyzed, Roosevelt refused to give up without a good fight. Many people, including his mother, said he should abandon his political career, but he was determined to get back on his feet. Following an extremely difficult exercise routine, he regained the use of most of his body. However he was never able to walk again without leg braces or someone's help.

May 12, 1936.

My dear Harold:
    I have your letter, telling me that you will have to spend your vacation in the hospital.
    I do hope that your stay there will be very helpful and that you may return home greatly improved.

My best wishes to you.
Very sincerely yours,

(Franklin Delano Roosevelt)

Harold Hancock

2135 North 67th Street,
St. Louis,
Missouri.

Perhaps photographers and other media people of the time feared that showing Roosevelt's condition would make him look weak to most Americans. In fact, Roosevelt and his wife, Eleanor, were respected and loved by the majority of the American people. Roosevelt died during his fourth term, having served longer than any other president. The letter from Harold Hancock and the president's reply show how serious and dreaded polio was in those years.

The last letter in this chapter is a surprise. It is written by a young boy whose native language is Spanish. Although his English is good for someone his age, it is still a little bit difficult to understand. Read it carefully and see if you recognize who the young author is and how we know him today.

Santiago de Cuba
Nov 6 1940.
Mr. Franklin Roosevelt,
President of the United States.

My good friend Roosevelt:
I don't know very English, but I know as much as write to you.
I like to hear the radio, and I am very happy, because I heard in it, that you will be President for a new (periodo)

I am twelve years old. I am a boy but I think very much but I do not think that I am writting to the President of the United States.

If you like, give me a ten dollars bill green american, in the letter, because never, I have not seen a ten dollars bill green american and I would like to have one of them.

My address is:
  Sr. Fidel Castro
  Colegio de Dolores.
  Santiago de Cuba
  Oriente. Cuba.

I don't know very English but I know very much Spanish and I suppose you don't know very Spanish but you know very English because you are American but I am not American.

Fidel Castro

If you want iron to build your ships I will show to you the bigest (minas) of iron of the land. They are in Mayari. Oriente Cuba

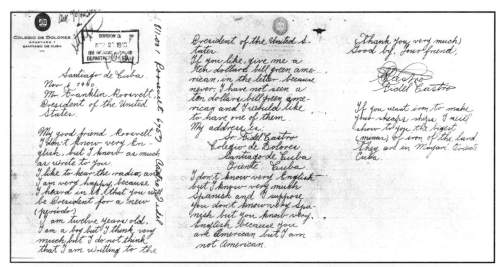

Santiago de Cuba.
Nov 6 1940.
Mr Franklin Roosevelt
President of the United
States.

My good friend Roosevelt
I don't know very En-
glish, but I know as much
as write to you.
I like to hear the radio, and
I am very happy, because
I heard in it, that you will
be President for a new
(periodo)
I am twelve years old.
I am a boy but I think very
much but I do not think
that I am writting to the

President of the United S-
tates.
If you like, give me a
ten dollars bill green american, in the letter, because
never, I have not seen a
ten dollars bill green american and I would like
to have one of them.
My address is:
Sr Fidel Castro
Colegio de Dolores
Santiago de Cuba
Oriente. Cuba.
I don't know very English
but I know very much
Spanish and I suppose
you don't know very Spa-
nish but you know very
English because you
are American but I am
not American.

(Thank you very much)
Good by. Your friend,

Fidel Castro

If you want iron to make
your sheaps ships, I will
show to you the biggest
(minas) of iron of the land.
They are in Mayari. Oriente
Cuba.

The young student whose letter to President Roosevelt appears here was Fidel Castro. He would later become the leader of the guerrilla forces that overthrew the Cuban dictator, Fulgencio Batista, in 1957. Castro is the bearded man in the center.

chapter 3
Another War and Lunch Counters

Many generations of young people have lived with the threat of a war or have lived through a war. Even if the wars were not fought on American soil, the nation's young people have been affected.

President Harry S. Truman served as vice president under Franklin D. Roosevelt during World War II. After only 83 days of experience as vice president, he succeeded to the presidency when Roosevelt died. Truman and the country were stunned by the loss of Roosevelt, but the new president had to get right to work because there was still a war on that had to be won. Unfortunately, he had not been part of Roosevelt's inner circle, so he had to be quickly briefed on the war situation. He faced the tremendous challenge of leading the country while being compared to such a forceful and well-loved president as Roosevelt. Truman's presidency was not an easy one, yet most historians, politicians, and the general public believe that he was a good president and leader as well as an honest, plainspoken man.

Although Germany was defeated in May 1945, Truman still had to make the awesome decision of whether or not to use the powerful new atomic bomb against Japan. Scientists, politicians, and the president hoped that using this destructive bomb against the Japanese would end World War II quickly and thus save soldiers' lives. Truman decided to use the bomb, and we now know how tragic the results were for the Japanese people.

When the war ended and the troops started coming home, Truman was faced with new problems. The United States had to shift from a wartime economy of making weapons and uniforms, and feeding the troops, to a peacetime one of producing homes, appliances, and cars for veterans and their families. Women who had worked in factories and offices during the war were told to go back to their kitchens because the returning soldiers needed the jobs.

President Harry S. Truman

Communism, a political, social, and economic system in which the state controls many aspects of life, was taking hold in some countries. With the start of the Cold War, a state of mistrust and hostility between the United

States and the Soviet Union, the world was once again divided along political lines. President Truman created government organizations to strengthen the nation, including the Department of Defense, the Central Intelligence Agency, and the National Security Council. He announced the Truman Doctrine, which promised American aid to nations resisting communism. During his administration, the North Atlantic Treaty Organization (NATO) was founded; it was an organization composed of the United States and eleven other nations that pledged to help each other. General Dwight D. Eisenhower, a hero of World War II, served as the first supreme commander of NATO forces. The United Nations was established in 1945 and later moved into its permanent headquarters in New York City. This was the first time the United States agreed to join a world organization designed to keep the peace.

By 1950, the United States was changing quickly. Television programs could now be seen coast to coast. Almost every American family owned a car.

In the peace negotiations after World War II, the Asian peninsula of Korea was divided, with a freely elected government in the south and a communist-controlled government in the north. On June 25, 1950, North Korean forces invaded South Korea. U.S. and United Nations forces defended South Korea and demanded that North Korea withdraw. Another World War II American hero, General Douglas MacArthur, commanded the U.N. forces in Korea, and by the fall of 1950 he had most of Korea under control. Then Chinese communist troops joined with the North Koreans and drove MacArthur's troops back toward South Korea.

Mr. Harry S. Truman
President of the United States
White House
Washington, D. C.

Dear Mr. Truman:

I am a student at Waynesboro High School, Waynesboro, Virginia. Our Geography class is now studying
the war in Korea, and we are going to make a scrap
book on this country. I should like your opinion of the
war to put in my scrap book.

Mr. Truman, it is very important that the boys and girls
in our schools know what is going on. I have a young
brother in Korea and I know what it means to be
afraid to read the paper, listen to the radio, or receive
mail-afraid that in any one of these we may hear that
he is dead or has been captured by a murderous group
of foreigners who will probably torture him to death.

We have had wars before, and never in the history of
our country have we lost one. We should like to know
what our chances are of winning this one. We already know that this is more serious than any war before, but we hope and pray that there is a chance.

I think, and I know you will agree, that we have a right to know what is going on, what our chances are, and when OUR BOYS will be home. We shall appreciate an answer to this letter so we will understand better our chances of winning or losing this frightening war.

Yours very truly,
(Miss) Florence Newcomb

239 Arch Avenue
Waynesboro, Virginia

The letter to Truman from Florence Newcomb expresses the fear many young people in the United States felt during the Korean War. Many of them had a brother, father, uncle, or friend involved in the war.

Truman wanted to limit the war to Korea, while MacArthur wanted to attack Chinese communist bases in Manchuria, in northeastern China. MacArthur made the mistake of disagreeing with his commander in chief —the president—and also talking about his views publicly. Truman dismissed MacArthur and ordered him to come home. Most Americans were upset about this. As you can see in the second Truman letter, even school-age young people were in a furor over the hero's dismissal. It was the topic of headlines and news programs all over the country.

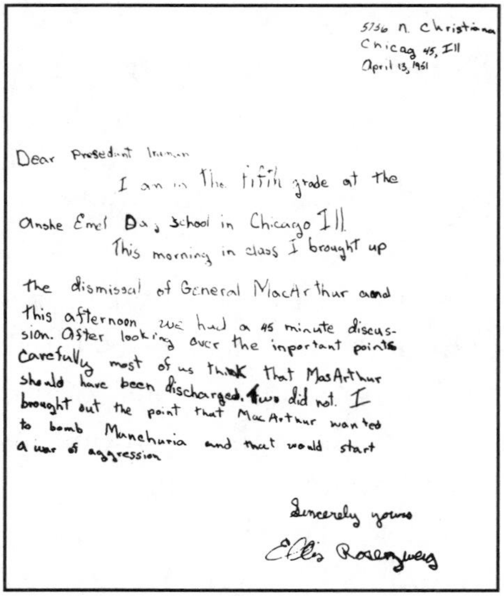

5736 N. Christiana
Chicag 45, Ill
April 13, 1951

Dear Presedent Truman:

I am in the fifth grade at the Anshe Emet Day School in Chicago Ill.

This morning in class I brought up the dismissal of General MacArthur and this afternoon we had a 45 minute discussion. After looking over the important points carefully most of us think that MacArthur should have been discharged. Two did not. I brought out the point that MacArthur wanted to bomb Manchuria and that would start a war of aggression.

Sincerely yours,
Ellis Rosenzweig

5736 N. Christiana
Chicag 45, Ill
April 13, 1951

Dear Presedent Truman

I am in the fifth grade at the Anshe Emet Day school in Chicago Ill.

This morning in class I brought up the dismissal of General MacArthur and this afternoon we had a 45 minute discussion. After looking over the inportant points carefully most of us think that MasArthur should have been discharged. Two did not. I brought out the point that MacArthur wanted to bomb Manchuria and that would start a war of aggression

Sincerely yours
Ellis Rosenzweig

President Truman traveled to Wake Island in the Pacific Ocean to meet with—and dismiss—General Douglas MacArthur.

On January 20, 1953, after completing his second term in office, Truman retired to his home in Independence, Missouri. The next American president was General Dwight D. Eisenhower, who defeated the Democratic candidate, Adlai Stevenson.

During Eisenhower's two terms as the 34th president of the United States, much of the world changed. Three years of bloody fighting in Korea ended with a truce in 1953. That year the U.S. Department of Health, Education, and Welfare was created. Also in 1953, Americans Ethel and Julius Rosenberg were accused of passing secret information about the atomic bomb to the Russians and were executed. Senator Joseph McCarthy led a frenzied search for communists in the United States government.

In the 1954 landmark case, *Brown v. Board of Education of Topeka,* the Supreme Court ordered an end to racial segrega-

President Dwight D. Eisenhower gives a televised public address before a state visit to the Far East.

tion in schools. The first nuclear power plant for peacetime use began operating in 1955. The space age officially began in 1957 when Russia launched the satellite Sputnik I. A year later the United States sent up its own first satellite, Explorer I. Between 1956 and 1961, 24 African nations won their independence. In 1958, U.S. airlines began the first jet passenger service. Alaska and Hawaii became the 49th and 50th states in 1959. Over 45 million Americans had televisions by 1960. While Eisenhower was president and Richard M. Nixon was vice president, the population of the United States was 181,700,000, and the minimum wage was increased to $1.00 per hour!

Many of Eisenhower's problems during his presidency centered on race relations at home. To integrate schools, following the 1954 Supreme Court decision, Eisenhower sent federal troops to Little Rock, Arkansas. The soldiers protected black students who were entering Central High School for the first time. Riots often broke out when black students tried to enter all-white schools and it took several years to get all schools to accept integration.

The two Eisenhower letters are very different. In the first, three young girls from Montana express their concern about the entertainer Elvis Presley going into the army. They especially don't want his long hair and sideburns cut! This letter can be found in Eisenhower's presidential library. It shows how much many young Americans adored the handsome singer and identified with his free and easy rock and roll songs. The letter was marked "file" at the top, meaning it was saved along with letters dealing with more serious topics, such as the second Eisenhower letter shown here.

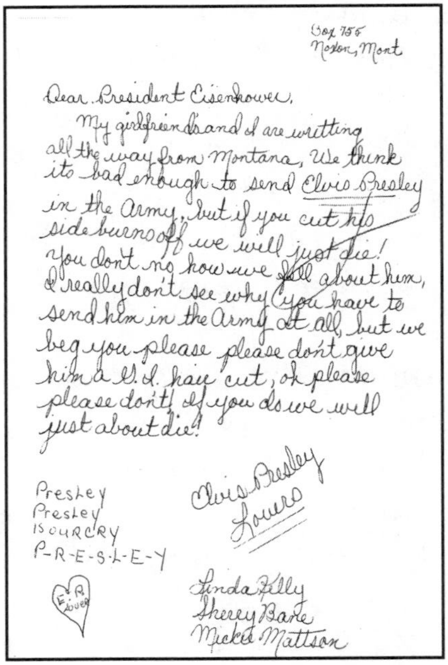

Box 755
Noxon, Mont.

Dear President Eisenhower,

My girlfriend's and I are writting all the way from Montana, We think its bad enough to send Elvis Presley in the Army, but if you cut his side burns off we will just die! You don't no how we fell about him, I really don't see why you have to send him in the Army at all, but we beg you please please don't give him a G.I. hair cut, oh please please don't! If you do we will just about die!

Elvis Presley Lovers
Presley
Presley
is our cry
P-R-E-S-L-E-Y

Linda Kelly
Sherry Bane
Mickie Mattson

Box 755
Noxon, Mont

Dear President Eisenhower,
My girlfriend's and I are writting all the way from Montana, We think its bad enough to send Elvis Presley in the Army, but if you cut his side burns off we will just die! You don't no how we fell about him, I really don't see why you have to send him in the Army at all, but we beg you please please don't give him a G.I. hair cut, oh please please don't! If you do we will just about die!

Presley
Presley
is our cry
P-R-E-S-L-E-Y

Elvis Presley Lovers

E.P. Lover

Linda Kelly
Sherry Bane
Mickie Mattson

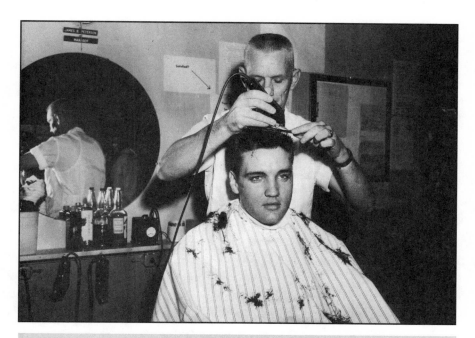

Newspapers around the world carried photographs of singer Elvis Presley receiving his first Army haircut at Fort Chaffee, Arkansas.

This letter was written by a young man from New York, and shows how concerned many northern students were about what was happening in the South, especially to people their age. Pedro Dummitt Jr. writes about the painful and embarrassing treatment many blacks endured, as they were refused service at lunch counters. He emphasizes that the Constitution covers individuals' rights to eat where they want and go to school where they wish. This young writer calls upon the president to be more honorable and fair about race relations, especially in the South. It is a thoughtful letter, and it reflects the feelings of millions of Americans during Eisenhower's presidency.

60 E. 135th St
New York 37, NY
March 18, 1960

Dear President Eisenhower,

I suppose you know about the Negroes in the South, and what a hard time they are having with whites students and eating at lunch counters. It seems as if you and the southern governments are not taking action on this situation.

If you were a Negro you wouldn't want this trouble to come upon you. According to the the Constitution everyone has their privilege to eat at lunch counters. No matter what race they're in. And this is not so in the "south." It's almost like there is slavery in the South (To Negro Students). You are a good President but you aren't being as fair as a honorable President is. Another thing the missile race or program, is not too good either.

What about the huge powered Jupiter-C. That is supposed to lead the way for the U.S.? Will it be a success? The way it looks now, it seems as if we never will catch up with Russia.

Yours Truly
Pedro A. Dummitt jr.

Lunch counter sit-in demonstrations against racial discrimination erupted in cities throughout the country. In this Oklahoma City drugstore, the protesters were allowed to sit at the counter, but were refused service.

chapter 4
What You Can Do for Your Country

Courage, patriotism, responsibility, glamour, and sadness all come to mind when President John F. Kennedy's name is mentioned. Elected president in 1960 after a tough campaign against former vice president Richard M. Nixon, Kennedy promised the American people a "New Frontier." His plans included raising the minimum wage, exploring space, and protecting civil rights.

In his inaugural address, he told Americans to "Ask not what your country can do for you—ask what you can do for your country." Americans were stirred by his words, his enthusiasm, and his youthful energy.

Kennedy, who was the 35th president, received a great deal of mail from young people, covering many different topics. A few letters appear in this chapter as examples of the concerns and fears of young Americans during the three years he held office before being assassinated in Dallas, Texas, in November 1963.

There were 50 states in the Union and about 190,000,000 Americans when Kennedy and his young family were in the

White House. He accomplished many important things during his presidency. Although he didn't "shut down the bar joints" as the first letter requests, Americans flew in space for the first time largely because Kennedy pushed the space program. In 1962, John Glenn became the first American to orbit the Earth. A treaty was signed by the United States, Russia, and other countries in 1963 which banned all but underground nuclear testing. The Freedom March brought about 200,000 African Americans and whites to Washington, D.C., to demand equal rights for people of color.

Bonnie Lee Williams
Route 5
Box 564
Monroe, North Carolina

President John. F. Kennedy
Washington

Dear Sir,
    I am in the 5th grade and I am 11 years old. I am writing to you about the Bars that are in the United States. I know that you do not have enough for a little girl like me but if you will please put a law against the beer joints. If you will I will repay you in all the way that I can. Please write to me and tell me if you will or will not.

Thank you,
Bonnie Lee Williams

President John F. Kennedy

One of Kennedy's long-lasting achievements was the establishment of the Peace Corps in 1961. This organization recruits and trains U.S. citizens to work in many less developed countries to help improve living conditions. After three-month training periods, the volunteers serve for three years, living in the same conditions as the people they are trying to help. Since the program was established, nearly 150,000 Americans have served in over 130 countries. Currently, more than 6,000 American volunteers and trainees are serving in 90 countries throughout the world.

John F. Kennedy's foreign policy efforts were not always totally successful. He could not stop the communists from building the Berlin Wall in 1961, thus sealing off the escape route from East Berlin to West Berlin. Also in 1961, Kennedy encouraged Cuban refugees living in the United States and who opposed the communist government led by Fidel Castro to invade the island nation and overturn its government. When the Cuban opposition forces landed at the Bay of Pigs, Castro's forces quickly captured them. The next year, Kennedy learned that the Russians were setting up missile sites in Cuba and ordered a naval blockade to keep Soviet

In 1962, President Kennedy greeted one of the first groups of Peace Corps trainees on the south lawn of the White House.

ships from entering Cuban ports. The Soviets backed down and removed the missiles from the island, which is very close to the United States. By 1963, the Kennedy administration was becoming increasingly involved in the ongoing conflict between North and South Vietnam.

The letter written by Joyce Smith expresses the mood of most teens during Kennedy's presidency. They had been stirred by his speeches and teachers had reinforced those feelings, yet just exactly what young adults should do was often a mystery to them. The answer from Ralph A. Dungan, special assistant to the president, tells how the government thought young adults could best be of help to their country.

In the 1960s, fear of gunfire and violence, as well as atomic war, troubled young people, as the letters from Sandra

59 Freehold Road
Englishtown, New Jersey
November 5, 1961

President John F. Kennedy
The White House
Washington, D. C.

Dear Mr. President:

I am a senior in Freehold Regional High School, Freehold, New Jersey. My Western Civilizations classmates and I have been the object of a number of lectures concerning what we are doing for our country.

Our teacher feels that the coming society had better get on-the-ball, or else they may someday live under Communism. He keeps stressing the point that we should do something. When the students ask what to do, he says work. I want to know what kind of work. Besides using our education facilities to the fullest extent, what else can the youth of America do?

I'm sure that no one in our great country would enjoy living under Communism. My fellow students and I want to know what type of work to do in order that we may serve our country better and keep it a free nation forever.

The main object of this letter is to find out what to do and how to work to preserve democracy in the coming society.

Respectfully yours,
Joyce Smith
November 27, 1961

Smith and Harriet Jisa show. Again Dungan answered with a letter that tried to help the writers be less fearful.

Overall, in a short time as president, Kennedy—with the help of Congress and the Supreme Court—accomplished many things for the American people. The minimum wage was raised, trade with Europe improved, and the growing demands of blacks for equal rights were beginning to be acknowledged. Kennedy asked Congress to pass laws requiring hotels, motels, and restaurants to serve people regardless of color. Desegregation of schools continued, and the hot line— a direct telephone link between Moscow and Washington— was established to reduce the risk of war.

On November 22, 1963, President Kennedy was assassinated in Dallas, Texas. Once it was announced that the president

November 27, 1961

Dear Miss Smith:

Thank you for your letter to the President and for the thoughtful interest which prompted you to ask what you can do for our country.

There are many ways you can be of service in our efforts to preserve our great heritage and to accept our role as leader in freedom's cause. I am enclosing releases which include some of the things the President has asked of us in this respect. There is also enclosed information on the People-to-People Program which I though you might like to have.

Sincerely,

Ralph A. Dungan
Special Assistant
to the President

was dead, Lyndon B. Johnson, the vice president, took the oath of office aboard the presidential air force jet with his wife, Ladybird, and Jacqueline, Kennedy's widow, beside him. For the next few days, Americans stayed glued to their televisions to watch the drama of the president's funeral. Families sat together and cried for what seemed to be the end of an era of beauty, culture, freedom, and responsibility.

13071 Relieance
Arleta, California
Sept. 27, 61
President Kennedy
White House
Washington, D.E.

Dear Sir,
   My name is Sandra Lynn Smith. I am ten (10) years old. I live in Los Angeles, California.
   Almost every night I have very bad dreams about a war, and even if I try to think about pleasant things, but war is in the backround. That is why I am writing. I would like you to write me what you think is going to happen.

Thank you,
Sandra Smith

P.P.S. I would like to know very badly

363 So Dos Caminos
Nov. 10, 1961

Dear President Kennedy,
    The last time I wrote you you were senator. Many things have changed haven't they. Are we in great danger of an atomic attack? I hope you will be able to help America. I am a little bit afraid. Do you think there will be a war? How can I help my country and my family and friends? I will try my best to help my country.

Your American friend,
Harriet Jisa

Lyndon Johnson, the 36th president, went to work to keep the country's concerns over the change in leadership at a minimum. Johnson had spent much of his life serving his country. He had been in the U.S. Navy during World War II, served in the House of Representatives, was elected to the U.S. Senate in 1948, and became vice president in 1960.

As a senator, he had urged the exploration of outer space and had been the first chairperson of the Senate Aeronautic and Space Committee. He was very well known and had a great deal of influence in the Senate.

December 18, 1961

Dear Harriet:

The President has asked me to thank you for your message. He is pleased to know that you are interested in our Nation's affairs, as this is a good indication that we will have well-qualified leaders in the future.

In reply to your query, you can best help by being studious and law-abiding. Acquiring all the education you can, including the study of other countries, is an important part of the responsibility of citizenship. This will make you more aware of our Nation's problems and you will be preparing yourself to share in their solution.

With the President's best wishes,

Sincerely,

Ralph A. Dungan
Special Assistant
to the President

Johnson faced many difficult problems as president, including the continuing cold war, fear of a nuclear war, serious racial tension, and high unemployment. The programs the president wanted passed were stuck in Congress, and more American soldiers were being sent to Vietnam to fight in the escalating conflict. The Vietnam War sharply divided Americans. Many people thought that we did not belong in such a war and that we should get our soldiers out. Others believed that we had to protect South Vietnam, an ally, to prevent its takeover by communist soldiers from the north. Widespread unrest marked the 1960s, as protesters pushed for social and political change through both peaceful demonstrations and violent rioting.

President Lyndon Johnson

President Johnson gave his attention to wiping out slums and poverty. He signed the Federal Aid to Education Act as part of his "Great Society" reforms. These reforms included giving more money to schools and establishing the Headstart programs and Medicare, a health plan for the elderly, which took effect in 1966. Sadly, two prominent Americans were assassinated in 1968: the Reverend Martin Luther King Jr. and Senator Robert F. Kennedy, brother of the previous president.

Johnson named the first African American person to the president's cabinet—Robert C. Weaver, who served as Secretary of Housing and Urban Development. Thurgood Marshall was the first black appointed to the Supreme Court. But problems at home increased by 1967, and Johnson's Great Society programs were not favored by the new Republicans elected to Congress.

The nation was shocked when Johnson declined to run for reelection in 1968. He felt he had become a symbol of the unrest and division at home.

The letter to Johnson in this chapter shows that in the

The Lyndon Baines Johnson Presidential Library is located on the University of Texas campus.

middle of this unrest and serious tension in the United States, young people's concerns weren't always about the war. They also weren't always things a president could resolve. However, using their democratic rights, these people wrote to the president to try to correct what they considered a wrong.

3034 Brighton St
Philadelphia, Pa 19149

Dear Mr. President,
　　In a newspaper recently there was an article saying that if the Beatles came in August the Music Union won't allow them to bring their instruments. It also stated that they needed government approval, will you please give that approval? I know your daughter likes them, although you may not, please do it for the teenagers of America!
I have a ticket to see them and so do many other teens and if they can't bring their instruments how are they going to perform? Will you Please tell the Union to disregard that statement? About 50 million teens will love you for it. Mr. Johnson you can't allow them to keep them or their instruments out of America, please, please do something, you stopped a train strike for a 7 yr. old girl, please do this for the teens of America, we will be eternily grateful.
Thank you!
Love,
Dellie Carey
P.S. Do you like them?

Fear that the Beatles—seen here on their first American tour in 1964—would not be allowed to bring their instruments into the country caused great alarm. Back row, from the left: Ringo Starr, John Lennon; front row: George Harrison, Paul McCartney

chapter 5
Going across Town

After Lyndon Johnson decided not to run for reelection, Richard M. Nixon finally got the chance he had craved for many years. As Eisenhower's vice president in 1952 and 1956, Richard Nixon had a great amount of experience in the workings of the White House, was skilled at foreign affairs, and knew most of the world's leaders. During periods when Eisenhower was ill, Nixon ran the U.S. government. He calmly carried out his duties, attended cabinet meetings, and generally kept the government running while Eisenhower recuperated from a heart attack and other serious illnesses. This gave Nixon more experience than most vice presidents get and convinced him that he should be elected president. But Kennedy defeated him in 1960, and Nixon did not take office as president until 1969, during a very troubled period in American history. At that time, the U.S. population was about 203,235,206.

The war in Vietnam had not yet ended. Many Americans just wanted the war to be over and the bloodshed stopped.

Others felt withdrawing American troops would look like a defeat. Nixon had made a campaign promise that, if elected, he would end the war, and voters seemed intent on holding him to that promise.

Another important issue on Nixon's agenda was race relations and the question of how to achieve school integration. The letter to Nixon in this chapter expresses one young woman's view on inte-

President Richard Nixon

gration and echoes the feelings of many other young people who were caught up in the political situation of the times.

Many advances were made during Nixon's presidency. Three American astronauts, Michael Collins, Neil Armstrong, and Buzz Aldrin, traveled through space to the moon. Americans watched their television sets with great pride and excitement as the moon vehicle touched down and Armstrong and Aldrin climbed out and actually stood on the moon!

The Nixon period was a time of some progress in areas of human rights and social equality. First, through the 26th Amendment, the voting age in the United States was lowered from 21 to 18. The Supreme Court approved busing as a way to end school segregation. Women's liberation, a movement aimed at winning equal opportunities for women in all areas

19 Elizabeth Avenue
Chickasaw, Alabama 36611
August 1, 1970

Dear PRESIDENT NIXON,
     I am 14 years old, my name is Sheri Caffman, and I am very interested in the School situation in the South.
     I would like to like to know why IcCAN NOT graduate from the high school in my neighborhood, instead of going across town to another high school as the Federal Judge said I would have to do.
     The people of Mobile District are very concerned about this situation.
     PRESIDENT NIXON, you are suppose to be our President too.
     So Please help us go to the school in our neighborhood.
     Please reply at your earliest convenience.

Sincerely Yours
Sheri Caffman

of life, gathered attention and supporters in the early 1970s. Title IX, which required that schools give girls equal time, facilities, and opportunities for sports, was signed by Nixon as part of an education act in 1972. Many of today's famous women athletes got their start because Nixon signed that bill. Many of you are on sports teams that did not exist before Title IX. The environment became a growing concern, and citizens who had been trying since the early 1960s to get something done about toxins, pollutants, and poisoned streams were relieved to have the Environmental Protection Agency established to tackle the pollution problems. The late 1960s and early 1970s also saw the gradual withdrawal from Vietnam of U.S. military forces. Nixon was also the first president to visit China while in office. The country had been closed to outsiders and it was not until 1971 that China joined the United Nations.

During Nixon's reelection campaign in 1972, some of his staff hired a number of people to break into the Democratic National Headquarters in the Watergate building in Washington, D.C. The burglars were caught while trying to set up eavesdropping equipment that would have let Republicans overhear Democratic campaign plans. Eventually, some members of Nixon's reelection committee were arrested and charged. Then, top White House aides were linked to the situation and finally Nixon himself was drawn into the scandal. Nixon had tapes of his conversations about the break-in, but he refused to turn them over to the Congress and the courts. The House Judiciary Committee held hearings from October 1973 until July 1974, when the committee voted to recommend that the president be charged with obstructing justice because he delayed the Watergate investigation, attempted to hide the identities of the people involved in the break-in and its planning, abused presidential powers, and disobeyed subpeonas (court orders for him to appear or give evidence).

Before the Senate could bring him to trial, as the Constitution requires, Nixon decided to resign. On August 9, 1974,

Richard Nixon went on national television to tell the nation that he would resign from the office of president of the United States. Gerald R. Ford was sworn in as the 38th president at noon on the same day.

One of Ford's first actions was to grant Nixon a pardon, forgiving him for any possible federal crimes. Ford hoped that the Watergate scandal would come to an end with this pardon and that people would trust the government once more. Coming into the presidency as he did, Ford faced a difficult job. Many people resented Nixon's pardon, as it looked as if a president could break the law and not be punished. Ford believed there were many ways to be punished and that Nixon's exile from politics was a devastating punishment for him. Apparently others agreed with Ford, as seen in the letter from Robert Lind. It shows how some young people viewed Nixon and Watergate.

Dear Mr. Ford, I think you did the right thig because he was an ok President. Some times he makes mistakes but evrewun makes mustackes.
from Robert Lind.

Ford was our nation's only nonelected president. He had been appointed vice president to replace Spiro Agnew, who had been forced to resign because he had accepted bribes. Now Ford was president only because Nixon resigned. He served out the remainder of Nixon's term, from 1974 to 1977. Ford came to the presidency when the country was suffering from a loss of public confidence in govern-

President Gerald Ford

ment, very high inflation, and a slowdown in business activity.

Ford was determined to turn around the problems of the country. He offered amnesty, or pardons, to those young people who had fled the country or otherwise evaded the draft during the Vietnam War. Ford introduced legislation to create public service jobs for unemployed people. He also asked Congress to vote for lower federal income taxes. Congress passed both measures and these helped the economy.

Twice there were assassination attempts on President Ford's life. Both assailants were women, who were sentenced to life in prison. Despite these two scary attempts on his life, Ford was an easygoing and relaxed president. He and his wife, Betty, entertained often in the White House and were known for their friendly hospitality.

In April 1975, the Vietnam War ended, with North Vietnam taking over South Vietnam. Ford arranged for the evacuation to the United States of about 100,000 people desperate to leave South Vietnam. In another tense situation, the *Mayaguez*, a U.S. merchant ship, was captured by Cambodian communist troops in 1975. President Ford sent in the U.S. Marines, who took back the ship and saved the lives of the 39 crew members.

Happier events during Ford's presidency included the tall sailing ships gliding into ports throughout the country to celebrate the nation's Bicentennial (200th anniversary) and the Viking I Spacecraft landing on Mars, the first space vehicle to land on that planet.

In the 1976 election, Gerald Ford was the Republican candidate. Although he had worked hard to restore Americans' faith in government, and to repair the damage of the Vietnam War and the Watergate scandal, many Americans were ready for a change. That change came about with the election of a down-home person, Jimmy Carter, the Democratic candidate who claimed to be an outsider, not a Washington politician.

chapter 6
Two Governors Became Presidents

As the governor of Georgia, Jimmy Carter was well known in his state. Outside of Georgia, however, few Americans knew his name in 1976. When he started his presidential campaign, some people laughed and said "Jimmy who?" This actually helped Carter win the Democratic nomination because many voters liked the idea that Carter had not served in Washington, D.C. He became a symbol of a leader who was not tied to groups of politicians or businesspeople. He owed no special favors to anyone. He also attracted support from people who liked his promise to be a moral leader.

Carter had been in politics for a long time in Georgia. As governor, he had begun a project to honor black Georgians by hanging their portraits in the state capitol. The portrait of the Reverend Martin Luther King Jr. was the first to be hung. As president, Carter continued to pay attention to the country's diverse population and to the needs of the poor. He pardoned the draft evaders of the Vietnam War period and established the Department of Energy. He tried to fight in-

President Jimmy Carter enjoyed talking to young visitors to the White House.

flation and create jobs as well as reduce the cost of running the government.

The letter to Carter from Kim Shapiro mentions several concerns of Americans during Carter's presidency. The city of New York was in financial trouble with very high unemployment. Large numbers of people were losing their jobs just as Kim's father had.

Carter was a caring president whose hard work led to several important accomplishments. In 1979, the United States

202 Crescent Ave
Leonia N.Y. 07605
Jan 21, 1977

Mr. J. Carter
1600 Pennsylvania Ave
Washington D.C.

Dear Mr President:
    I am very glad that you are President. Now to give you some ideas. I think you should do something about New York City going bankrupt and all those people getting laid off. I am just 12 years old so I dont know many thing's that are happing. I think you will be a very good President. The reason I am telling you about New York City and the people who are being laid off is because my father was a teacher in New York and he got laid off. And I think you should do something about the Japanese killing the whales. My brother is very much against it. I think you will be the best President ever.

Yours Truly,

Kim Shapiro

and China strengthened ties by establishing full diplomatic relations. That year also marked the end of 31 years of war between Israel and Egypt. In 1978, President Carter had helped work out the peace treaty which was signed in 1979, by Egyptian president Anwar Sadat and Israeli prime minister Menachem Begin.

Other events in 1979 caused great distress. That year saw the beginning of the 444-day captivity of more than 60 Americans who were held hostage in Iran. It was also the year of a nuclear power plant accident at Three Mile Island in Pennsylvania, which caused Americans to doubt the safety of nuclear energy. Because the Soviets invaded Afghanistan in 1979, Americans boycotted the 1980 summer Olympic games in Moscow as a protest.

During his presidency, Carter worked closely with Margaret Thatcher, the first woman prime minister of England. American women graduated from U.S. military academies for the first time in 1980.

Carter was an easygoing, informal, and kind man. His response to the letter from Frank Badame shows that he hesitated to hurt people's feelings. Even this letter got a kind reply from Carter.

Carter did not win a second term as president. Americans seemed to change their minds about the qualities they wanted in the person running the country. The Republicans nominated Ronald W. Reagan, former governor of California, as their candidate for president. Reagan charged that Carter had failed to deal with the problems of high inflation and unemployment. The American people had seemed eager to have a different type of president, but now chose one who was more formal and acted and looked more as they felt a president should.

Jimmy Carter returned to Georgia after his defeat. He and his wife, Roslyn, have written books and devoted much of

112 North contry Rd.
Shoreham New York 11786
February 16, 1977

Dear Mr. President,
    I sent you a letter of congratulation and you told "Anne Higgins" to answer me That makes me mad, Mr. President because it said you couldn't answer me unless I was 100 years old or married 50 years. Since I am eleven years old, you might not be in office by the time I am 100 year old. The way I see it you wasted money on a stamp, paper and envelope to say "you couldn't say hello". I look forward to an answer, because I am insulted. And I would like to hear what you have to say.

Sincerely,
Frank Badame

To Frank Badame –
Best Wishes - & thanks for your letter –
   Jimmy Carter

President Ronald Reagan

their time to projects to assist the poor and needy, and to help communities learn to help themselves throughout the United States and the world.

Ronald Reagan was inaugurated as the 40th president on January 20, 1981, with the former ambassador to the United Nations George Bush as the vice president. The population of the United States was about 226,542,203. At age 69, Reagan was the oldest man to become president. He was also the first movie star. During his two terms in office, the popular Reagan helped to raise the nation's spirits. With his movie and television experience, he could make any speech sound terrific and full of hope.

Reagan worked hard to fulfill his campaign promises, especially to strengthen the economy. His plan included a large increase in military spending, cuts in taxes, and welfare reform. Newspapers and magazines called his economic plan Reaganomics. This economic strategy worked at first, but it ended in failure. Although the economy began to recover again in the mid-1980s, Reagan received much loud and angry criticism.

His major critics included women, African Americans,

and environmentalists. Although Reagan appointed the first female Supreme Court Justice, Sandra Day O'Connor, and three women served in his cabinet, most women felt that was not enough. They wanted more important positions for women in government. African-American families were hardest hit by unemployment and the reduction in social programs, which were results of Reaganomics. Environmentalists opposed Reagan's efforts to weaken laws designed to protect air and water quality.

Andy Smith
400 London Pride Road
Irmo, South Carolina 29063

April 18, 1984

Dear Mr. President,
 My name is Andy Smith. I am a seventh grade student at Irmo Middle School, in Irmo, South Carolina.
 Today my mother declared my bedroom a disaster area. I would like to request federal funds to hire a crew to clean up my room. I am prepared to provide the initial funds if you will provide matching funds for this project.
 I know you will be fair when you consider my request. I will be awaiting your reply.

Sincerely yours,

Andy Smith

May 11, 1984

Dear Andy:

I'm sorry to be so late in answering your letter but, as you know, I've been in China and found your letter here upon my return.

Your application for disaster relief has been duly noted but I must point out one technical problem: the authority declaring the disaster is supposed to make the request. In this case, your mother.

However, setting that aside, I'll have to point out the larger problem of available funds. This has been a year of disasters: 539 hurricanes as of May 4th and several more since, numerous floods, forest fires, drought in Texas and a number of earthquakes. What I'm getting at is that funds are dangerously low.

May I make a suggestion? This Administration, believing that government has done many things that could better be done by volunteers at the local level, has sponsored a Private Sector Initiatives Program, calling upon people to practice voluntarism in the solving of a number of local problems.

Your situation appears to be a natural. I'm sure your mother was fully justified in proclaiming your room a disaster. Therefore, you are in an excellent position to launch another volunteer program to go along with the more than 3000 already underway in our nation. Congratulations.

Give my best regards to your mother.

Sincerely,

(Ronald Reagan)

In foreign affairs, the president dealt with strife in Lebanon and Israel. There were also rebellions in Nicaragua and El Salvador in the early 1980s. When rebels on the island of Grenada overthrew their government in 1983, the president sent in troops to protect the hundred Americans attending Grenadian medical school.

The presidential campaign of 1984 was noteworthy for two reasons. First, there were no real issues. The Democrats nominated Walter F. Mondale, who criticized Reagan's economic policy, but Reagan just talked about America "standing tall" once again. The second noteworthy aspect of the campaign was that Mondale chose a woman to be his vice presidential running mate. Geraldine Ferraro, a representative from New York, made history by being the first woman on the presidential ticket of a major political party.

The popular team of Reagan and Bush won the election with ease. Reagan's economic plans remained the same, and he was determined to build up the military even further. Reagan also worked to end the problems between the United States and the former Soviet Union. The eased tensions resulted in the signing of an arms control agreement with the Soviet leader Mikhail Gorbachev.

Although he had many critics, Reagan remained popular. He had a reassuring leadership style and he kept the image of a kindly grandfather. Yet at the end of his presidency, the goal of reducing the size of government had not been met and he had shifted priorities from such issues as child care and environmental protection to weapons buildup.

People who worked with Reagan say he had a wonderful sense of humor and cared for the people around him. These traits are seen in his answer to 12-year-old Andy Smith, who wanted money to clean up his room. Although Reagan had been in China working on foreign affairs, he took the time after his return to respond to this letter. Reagan's answer shows his gentle humor and an understanding of Andy's pride. Andy's letter is another example of how young people feel comfortable writing to the leader of their country and actually expect the letter to be read and answered.

When Ronald Reagan and his wife, Nancy, left Washington for retirement in California, polls indicated that he was a very popular president. In 1994, it was announced that the president was suffering from Alzheimer's disease, an illness characterized by a progressive deterioration of memory and other mental activity. He is now rarely seen in public.

chapter 7
Patriotism and Pride

After serving eight years as Ronald Reagan's vice president, George Bush moved into the White House as the 41st president on January 20, 1989. Bush and his wife, Barbara, were already well known to the American public. Some people think that Barbara's gentle, grandmotherly appeal helped get George elected. In spite of their differences, Reagan and Bush had worked well together. Bush had been one of the most widely traveled vice presidents, as Reagan sent him to many countries to represent the United States. In fact, he traveled over a million miles and visited over 75 countries as special representative of the president.

Bush's earlier experiences and jobs had also given him an impressive record. During World War II, Bush was the navy's youngest bomber pilot. He was shot down over the Pacific island of Chichi Jima and rescued by a submarine. Before the war ended, Bush had been awarded the Distinguished Flying Cross and three air medals. In 1967, he represented Houston, Texas, in the U.S. House of Representatives and voted for the Civil Rights Act of 1968, even though many of his constituents were against the new law. Bush was also the U.S. ambassador to the United Nations (1971-73) and then was head of the Central Intelligence Agency under President Ford from 1976 to 1977.

As president, Bush handled foreign affairs well but was less expert in domestic areas. He took advantage of the crumbling situation in some communist countries and negotiated a treaty with the former Soviet Union to reduce nuclear arms and other weapons.

President George Bush

George Bush sent military troops to Panama to depose its president, Manuel Noriega, because he was a dictator and a drug lord. Then in August 1990, Iraq invaded and took over the oil-rich country of Kuwait. In response, Bush sent more than 541,000 American troops to the Persian Gulf. Massive bombings and a swift ground attack by a combined force of Western and Arab troops routed the Iraqis in February 1991. The United Nations imposed a cease-fire in April 1991. Although Bush had tried to keep the news media away from the Gulf War by calling for a blackout, Americans could actually see glimpses of the war on television news stations. Broadcasts showed the missiles, tanks, bombers, and other technologically advanced weapons, such as the Tomahawk cruise missile and the Patriot antiaircraft system, in use. It seemed unreal, as if it were just a big video game, but it was a serious war led by General Norman Schwarzkopf, and many real people were killed. Many American soldiers are now suffering from strange diseases that may have been caused by the Gulf War.

On the home front, Bush shied away from the big issues. Issues such as the federal deficit and a poor economy dogged him throughout his presidency. One issue that he felt passionately about was the proper treatment of the U.S. flag. He wanted a constitutional amendment to outlaw desecration (destruction or disrespect) of the flag. Some political leaders felt that Bush was using the flag issue to get support from Americans. The amendment was never passed, but many Americans were concerned about ensuring respect for this symbol of our country. In the letters written by Chad Aylestock and his father, we can see how one young person felt about the flag. The letter was prompted by a cartoon that seemed to mock the flag.

The Doonesbury cartoon that sparked a controversy

Bush was known for answering his mail and writing to many people. His response to Chad and his father is typical in that he makes the person who wrote to him feel very important through his reply.

The 1992 election pitted Bush, a Republican, against Arkansas governor Bill Clinton, a Democrat. Clinton ran a successful campaign. He appeared smooth, sincere, up-to-date on issues, and his youthful and well-groomed appearance helped him look presidential. He walked into crowds of

President George Bush
The White House
Washington, D.C. 20500

Dear Mr. President,
    Thank you, sir, for giving a portion of your life to promote freedom and prosperity for the American people. May God give you wisdom, strength and the support of the American people.
    My son, Chad, read the enclosed "Doonesbury" comic which was printed in the Sunday, November 5, 1989, Washington Post. He then wrote the enclosed letter and mailed it to the editor of the Washington Post. Chad's letter was unsolicited by myself and was written entirely by himself. I though his letter might brighten your day.

    Thank you again.

Sincerely yours,
Wm. Michael Aylestock

admirers and shook hands. He laughed and told stories, spoke softly to each person and made each voter who met him feel special. Bush was the older man who didn't seem to be able to keep up with Clinton. He appeared to be copying Clinton's example, but never with the same grace or ability. Bill Clinton became the 42nd president and took the oath of office in January 1993.

To the _Washington Post_

To Whom it May Concern,
    I am a thirteen year old boy who moved from Canada about a year ago. I'm now a dual citizen + very patriotic. My family gets the Sunday paper. I was reading the Comics from Sunday 11-5-89, when I came upon the Doonesbury cartoon. Its not one of my favorite but I saw the flag on it and read it. I was very disgusted!!!!!! Also, in this comic strip, before this particular Sunday there have been some other cartoons that made me sick. Even though you are the Washington Post, you have no respect for our country, or our President. That flag is our national symbol and should not be joked about in this way. I hope you will consider what you put in your paper next time something like that comes up.

Sincerely yours,
Chad Aylestock

Clinton began his time in office focusing on such issues as gays in the military and on finding ways to appoint more African Americans and women to top positions in government. Two women he appointed are Janet Reno and Ruth Bader Ginsburg. Reno, the first female U.S. attorney general, is a graduate of Cornell University and Harvard Law School. She had won five terms in office as the attorney general of Florida before coming to Washington, D.C. Ruth Bader Ginsburg was a judge on the United States Court of Appeals for the District of Columbia. Bill Clinton nominated her

The White House
Washington
December 13, 1989

Dear Mr. Aylestock:

Thank you for sending me a copy of the letter your
son sent to The Washington Post. The sentiments he
expressed speak well of his upbringing.

Since I proposed a Constitutional Amendment to pro-
hibit desecration of our flag, I have heard from many of
our fellow citizens on both sides of this issue. The patriotism your son displays further convinces me that
we as a nation must preserve the flag as a symbol of
the honor, freedom, and justice so many Americans
fought for and died to defend. To dishonor the flag is to
dishonor them; I am determined not to let that happen.

I appreciate your son's actions and am glad you took
the time to inform me of them. Your letter did indeed
brighten my day. Barbara joins me in sending our best
wishes to you and Chad.

Sincerely,

(George Bush)

to the Supreme Court, making her the second woman in history to serve on the Court. Justice Ginsburg is known as a pioneer in the movement for legal equality of women and has written many books and articles on women's issues and legal rights.

Clinton seemed less experienced and decisive in responding to crises in Bosnia, Somalia, and Haiti, where internal warfare or the actions of a cruel dictator were causing great suffering. Clinton did however, push for the North American Free Trade Agreement (NAFTA), which was meant to phase out tariffs between the United States and its neighbors, Mexico and Canada. Congress was split over NAFTA with most Democrats against it and Republicans for it.

President Bill Clinton spoke at the Morgan State University commencement ceremonies in 1997.

Congress and the president worked successfully together on legislation making it easier to register to vote, allowing workers with newborn children or sick family members to take leave without pay, and giving financial aid to college students who perform national service work. Clinton also urged Congress to require a waiting period and a background check for prospective handgun buyers. He helped cut income taxes. He also supported efforts to get more police officers out on the streets and to build more prisons.

Despite questions about his trustworthiness and character, the steady growth in the economy helped Clinton be re-elected in 1996. For the second time, Al Gore of Tennessee was his vice president.

Both Clinton and Gore are often asked to speak to groups or schools. Their wives, Hillary Clinton and Tipper Gore, also address groups and organizations. With so many requests, Clinton and his staff must carefully select where he speaks. In 1996, Clinton was invited to speak at many high school, college, and university graduations. To prepare a campus for the president's arrival takes about three weeks, with the Secret Service and school administrators working together. It is a difficult process because many people attend the graduation, and it is important to keep the president safe from harm and on his time schedule. Clinton and his staff selected three graduation ceremonies. He appeared at his daughter Chelsea's high school graduation, at West Point Military Academy, and at Morgan State University, a small university in Baltimore, Maryland. Morgan is part of the Maryland state college system and is the only historically African-American college in Maryland. It was celebrating its 130th anniversary. The letters written by two undergraduates who heard his speech show how much his visit impressed them. The students speak of their pride in their school and the honor they felt when it was announced that Clinton would come to Morgan State University. Each thanked him for coming to their school and thereby showing that he cares about students, even those at small colleges. Such appearances are an important part of any president's job because young people look to him as a role model. They also see him as a celebrity and having him come to visit their campus is a treat.

Baltimore, MD 21239
July 29, 1997

Dear President Clinton,

My name is Monifa Elcock and I am a business student at Morgan State University. This letter is in response to the commencement address you delivered on May 18th to the class of 1997.

I would like to say "Thank you" for many reasons. First because you chose to speak at my school. Many prestigious universities would have loved to have you at their commencement ceremonies, and you chose to accept the invitation from Morgan State. My second reason is because I am grateful to you for recognizing the excellence of Morgan State University and the talent that it continues to produce. As a student, it means a great deal to hear your president say, "not only is your school a great historically black university, but a great American university." The third and main reason why I felt compelled to write you is to let you know that you have personally inspired me as a student. In the past, I have received Presidential Awards of Excellence from school, but your gesture has affected me personally. Watching you on the stage gave me a feeling that will never fade. So again, to you, President Clinton, I say thank you.

While I still have your attention, this would be a good time to remind you about the pledge you made to everyone who heard or read about your speech. You stated that "by the year 2000, every child, rich or poor, will have access to the same technology in the classrooms and libraries, by way of the Internet." Now, you only have three years left, and that statement is one that I plan to hold you to. I am still in college, but if you would like some volunteers to help you get started, I am available, and I think you would have no problem finding other volunteers at Morgan State University.

In addition to providing a fine education, Morgan State is a university that instills cultural pride in its students. We accept as our obligation the need to keep our cultural traditions alive—to show that there are African-American role models in classrooms and in business, in addition to the Michael Jordans and Tiger Woods of the world.

Now, I know that I would be pushing it if I asked you to come back to Morgan and speak at my graduation, too, but I would like to ask a favor. If I am ever invited by Morgan State University to speak as an alumnus at a commencement ceremony, I would be honored if you would attend as my guest. Then you will know that you played a very important role in the life of a student and are deserving of a pat on the back.

Yours Respectfully,
Monifa Elcock

Baltimore, MD 21239   07/28/97

Good Morning President Clinton:

My name is Marissa Lynch. I am a student at Morgan State University majoring in civil engineering, branching off into environmental engineering. I am entering my junior year and so far continuous hard work is helping me achieve my goal.

I would like to thank you for coming to Morgan and to commend you on the speech you delivered to the class of 1997 on May 18th. Your speech was uplifting and beneficial to the incoming students, the undergraduates, and the graduating class.

I appreciated the way you focused on Morgan as one of the most outstanding black colleges today. I was glad that you spoke about the great African Americans who graduated from Morgan and the courage they needed to overcome hatred.

It was important to talk about unemployment being the lowest in twenty-four years, the budget, and moving people off of welfare. But I was especially pleased that you stressed the cleaning up of the environment, cutting down on violence and, most important, that everyone should obtain a proper education. I am hopeful that scientists will succeed in finding a cure for AIDS within ten years.

I believe that people should follow your four guidelines. "Science should produce a better life for all and not few; Science should honor the tradition of equal treatment under law; Science should respect the privacy and autonomy of individuals, and Science should not be confused with faith in technology, and with faith in God."

I believe you are a man of your word. As you said, "Dream large. Work hard. We can do it." For me success comes by striving and working hard. We need to make this world a better place.

Yours Respectfully,

Marissa Lynch

chapter 8
Do You Want to Be President

Presidential campaigns vary dramatically, yet some themes do recur. History shows that the state of the economy and whether or not the country is at war are the two most critical issues for voters. They are also the two issues that come up most often in young people's letters to the president.

Although an election is the normal method of selecting a president and vice president, assassinations, resignations, and other unexpected events can result in a person becoming president who was not elected to that position. The 25th Amendment to the Constitution outlines the procedure to be followed if a vacancy occurs in either office, or if the president is incapacitated (unable to perform the duties of the office). If the presidency and vice presidency become vacant at the same time, the Speaker of the House of Representatives and the president pro tempore of the Senate are next in line, in that order, for the presidency.

The presidency is such a difficult job that many Americans wonder why anyone would want to do it. Yet many people have campaigned hard and spent a great deal of money to gain this position of leadership. Most of our presidents have been good leaders, and the letters young people write demonstrate their faith in these presidents. Leading the American nation forward is a challenge that attracts many men and women, and the power that comes with that office is indeed awesome.

You may decide to write a letter to the president. Perhaps you will have the opportunity to elect the first female president. It is important to write and vote so you can voice your opinions and exercise your rights as a citizen of a democracy. Have you ever thought about being president? If someday you hold this position, then young people will write to you about their concerns. How would you like the job of being the leader of the United States?

In addition to writing to the president, the public is also able to visit the president's residence, the White House.

Presidential Libraries and Selected Historic Sites and Museums

PRESIDENTIAL LIBRARIES

Herbert Hoover Library
Parkside Drive
P.O. Box 488
West Branch, IA 52358
(319) 643-5301
E-mail: library@hoover.nara.gov

Franklin D. Roosevelt Library
511 Albany Post Road
Hyde Park, NY 12538
(914) 229-8114
E-mail: library@roosevelt.nara.gov

Harry S. Truman Library
U.S. Highway 24 & Delaware Street
Independence, MO 64050-1798
(816) 833-1400
E-mail: library@truman.nara.gov

Dwight D. Eisenhower Library
S.E. Fourth Street
Abilene, KS 67410
(913) 263-4751
E-mail:
library@eisenhower.nara.gov

John Fitzgerald Kennedy Library
Columbia Point
Boston, MA 02125
(617) 929-4545
(617) 929-4500
E-mail: library@kennedy.nara.gov

Lyndon Baines Johnson Library
2313 Red River Street
Austin, TX 78705
(512) 482-5137
(512) 916-5137
E-mail: library@johnson.nara.gov

Nixon Presidential Materials Staff*
8601 Adelphi Road
College Park, MD 20740-6001
(301) 713-6950
E-mail: nixon@arch2.gov

Gerald R. Ford Library
1000 Beal Avenue
Ann Arbor, MI 48109-2114
(313) 744-2218
E-mail: library@fordlib.nara.gov

Jimmy Carter Library
441 Freedom Parkway &
One Copenhill Avenue

88

Atlanta, GA 30307
(404) 331-3942
E-mail: library@carter.nara.gov

Ronald Reagan Library
40 Presidential Drive
Simi Valley, CA 93065
(805) 522-8511
(805) 522-8444
E-mail: library@reagan.nara.gov

Bush Presidential Library and
Museum
1000 George Bush Drive
College Station, TX 77802
(409) 260-9552

*A Nixon library and museum is
maintained by a private organization. See the section on historic
sites for additional information.

SELECTED HISTORIC SITES
AND MUSEUMS

Here are the addresses of historic
sites or collections of presidents
who do not have libraries under
the jurisdiction of the National
Archives and Records Administration. Research collections at these
sites include primary and sec-
ondary source material.

George Washington
Mount Vernon
Mount Vernon Ladies Association
Mount Vernon, VA 22212
(703) 780-2000
E-mail: mountvernon.org

John Adams/John Quincy Adams
Adams National Historic Site
P.O. Box 531
Quincy, MA 02269
(617) 773-1177
E-mail: ADAM-Visitor-
Center@nps.gov

Thomas Jefferson
Monticello
P.O. Box 316
Charlottesville, VA 22902
(804) 293-2158

James Madison
Montpelier
P.O. Box 67
Montpelier Station, VA 22957
(703) 672-2728

James Monroe
Ash Lawn
James Monroe Parkway
Charlottesville, VA 22902
(804) 293-8000

Andrew Jackson
The Hermitage
4580 Rachel's Lane
Hermitage, TN 37076
(615) 889-2941

Martin Van Buren
Lindenwald
P.O. Box 545
Kinderhook, NY 12106
(518) 758-9265

William H. Harrison
Grouseland
3 W. Scott Street
Vincennes, IN 47591
(812) 882-2096

John Tyler
Sherwood Forest Plantation
P.O. Box 8
Charles City, VA 23030
(804) 829-2947

James K. Polk
James K. Polk Memorial State Historic Site
P.O. Box 475
Pineville, NC 28134
(704) 889-7145

Zachary Taylor
2102 Community Lane
Midland, TX 79710
(915) 682-2931

Millard Fillmore
Millard Fillmore House
P.O. Box 472
East Aurora, NY 14052
(716) 652-4228

Franklin Pierce
Pierce Homestead

P.O. Box 896
Hillsborough, NH 03244
(603) 478-3913

James Buchanan
James Buchanan Foundation for
the Preservation of Wheatland
1120 Marietta Avenue
Lancaster, PA 17603
(717) 392-8721

Abraham Lincoln
Lincoln Home National Historic
Site
413 Eighth Street
Springfield, IL 62701-1905
(217) 492-4150

Andrew Johnson
Andrew Johnson National Historic
Site
P.O. Box 1088
Greenville, TN 37743
(615) 638-3551

Ulysses S. Grant
Grant's Birthplace State Memorial
U.S. 52 & State Route 232
Point Pleasant, OH 45163
(513) 553-4911

Rutherford B. Hayes
Rutherford B. Hayes Presidential Center
Spiegel Grove
Fremont, OH 43420
(419) 332-2081

James A. Garfield
James A. Garfield National Historic Site
8095 Mentor Avenue
Mentor, OH 44060
(216) 255-8722

Chester A. Arthur
President Chester A. Arthur
Historic Site
135 State Street
Drawer 33
Montpelier, VT 05633-1201
(802) 828-3226

Grover Cleveland
Grover Cleveland Birthplace
207 Bloomfield Avenue
Caldwell, NJ 07006
(201) 226-8110

Benjamin Harrison
President Benjamin Harrison
Memorial Home
1230 N. Delaware Street
Indianapolis, IN 46202-2598
(317) 631-1898

William McKinley
The McKinley National Memorial
P.O. Box 20070
Canton, OH 44701
(216) 455-7043

Theodore Roosevelt
Sagamore Hill National Historic Site
20 Sagamore Hill Road
Oyster Bay, NY 11771-1899
(516) 922-4788

William H. Taft
William H. Taft National Historic Site
2038 Auburn Avenue
Cincinnati, OH 45219
(513) 684-3262

Woodrow Wilson
Woodrow Wilson Birthplace and
Museum
P.O. Box 24
Staunton, VA 24401
(703) 885-0897

Warren G. Harding
Harding Home and Museum
380 Mt. Vernon Avenue
Marion, OH 43302
(614) 387-9630

Calvin Coolidge
Forbes Library–Calvin Coolidge
Memorial Room
20 West Street
Northampton, MA 01060
(413) 584-6037

Richard M. Nixon
Richard M. Nixon Birthplace &
Museum
18001 Yorba Linda Boulevard
Yorba Linda, CA 92686
(714) 993-3393
E-mail: stedman@chapman.edu
Website:
http://www.chapman.edu/nixon

For More Information

Books

De Gregorio, William A. *The Complete Book of U.S. Presidents.* New York: Barricade Books, 1994.

Fradin, Dennis Brindell. *From Sea to Shining Sea: Washington, D.C.* Chicago: Children's Press, 1993.

Holms, John Pynchon. *The American Presidents: From Washington to Clinton.* New York: Pinnacle Books, 1996.

Montgomery, L.M. *Across the Miles: Tales of Correspondence.* New York: Bantam Books, 1995.

Quiri, Patricia Ryon. *The White House.* New York: Franklin Watts, 1996.

Sandler, Martin. *Presidents.* Washington, D.C.: A Library of Congress Book/Harper Collins, 1995.

Whitney, David C. *The American Presidents.* New York: Readers Digest, 1985.

Other Sources

To call the White House for information on how young people 18 and under can send letters to the president: (202) 456-7734.

The National Archives and Records Administration in Washington, D.C., maintains the personal papers, records, and memorabilia of the last 11

presidents of the United States. To reach the website of the National Archives and Records Administration for information on presidential libraries and sites:
http://www.nara.gov

The Library of Congress holds papers of 23 presidents on microfilm in the Manuscript Division. They also have many sites on the World Wide Web. You can access them with the following:
http://www.loc.gov
http://lcwebloc. gov/lcweb@loc.gov

For assistance on access and the contents of the collections, write to:

Library of Congress
Manuscript Division
Washington, D.C. 20540-4783
(202) 707-5387

The National Park Service and many private organizations oversee historic sites and museums associated with presidents.

Index